Lewis and Clark

History Maker Bios

Candice Ransom

L LERNER PUBLICATIONS COMPANY • MINNEAPOLIS

For my good friend Vicki

Maps on pp. 10 and 41 by Laura Westlund
Illustrations by Tim Parlin

Text copyright © 2003 by Candice Ransom
Illustrations copyright © 2003 by Lerner Publications Company
Reprinted in 2006

Lerner Publications Company
A division of Lerner Publishing Group
241 First Avenue North
Minneapolis, MN 55401 U.S.A.

Website address: www.lernerbooks.com

Library of Congress Cataloging-in-Publication Data

Ransom, Candice, 1952–
    Lewis and Clark / by Candice Ransom.
        p.   cm. — (History maker bios)
    Includes bibliographical references and index.
    Contents: Early roots—The Corps of Discovery—Up the Missouri—Meeting
the Shoshone—Homeward bound.
    ISBN-13: 978–0–8225–0394–1 (lib. bdg. : alk. paper)
    ISBN-10: 0–8225–0394–8 (lib. bdg. : alk. paper)
    1. Lewis, Meriwether, 1774–1809—Juvenile literature. 2. Clark, William,
1770–1838—Juvenile literature. 3. Explorers—West (U.S.)—Biography—
Juvenile literature. 4. Lewis and Clark Expedition (1804–1806)—Juvenile
literature. [1. Lewis, Meriwether, 1774–1809. 2. Clark, William, 1770–1838.
3. Explorers. 4. Lewis and Clark Expedition (1804–1806)] I. Title. II. Series.
F592.7 .R36 2003
917.804'2'0922—dc21   2002003265

Manufactured in the United States of America
2 3 4 5 6 7 – JR – 11 10 09 08 07 06

TABLE OF CONTENTS

INTRODUCTION

In 1801, most Americans lived within fifty miles of the Atlantic Ocean. Many people, including President Thomas Jefferson, dreamed of exploring the western part of the country. There were tales of mighty rivers and strange animals in the West. American Indians hunted and lived in this land of wonders.

In addition, America needed a trade route to the Pacific Ocean. Meriwether Lewis and William Clark were chosen to find the route.

Lewis and Clark were the first white Americans to cross the Rockies. They did not know what would happen on their trip, or if they would make it back. They had the courage to do it anyway.

This is their story.

1 EARLY ROOTS

Eight-year-old Meriwether Lewis often hunted in the middle of the night, wading through snow and icy streams. Meriwether liked to roam the fields and woods of Locust Hill, the Lewis family's estate. He had been born there in 1774. Locust Hill was in Virginia, near Thomas Jefferson's home.

The young boy and the great patriot sometimes gazed at the mountains of western Virginia. Both wondered what lay beyond them.

On the other side of the mountains, in Kentucky, another boy fished and hunted. His name was William Clark. His older brother, George Rogers Clark, had been a famous general in the Revolutionary War.

In 1789, nineteen-year-old William joined the army, too. He learned to draw maps, build forts, and sail boats. William also learned to travel safely through dangerous Indian country.

The Blue Ridge Mountains, part of the Appalachian Mountains, kept some early Virginians from traveling farther west.

When Meriwether Lewis was eighteen, he took over running Locust Hill. But he was bored tending crops. He missed wandering the countryside. When he was twenty, Meriwether joined the army. The captain of Meriwether's rifle company was red-haired William Clark. William was four years older than Meriwether. The two men became good friends.

Meriwether Lewis, as a young man

President Thomas Jefferson wanted the United States to expand.

William left the army in 1796. Meriwether stayed in the army another four years. He steered keelboats—large, shallow boats used to haul supplies—down the Ohio River. He explored the western territory and worked with Indian guides.

In 1801, Thomas Jefferson became the third president of the United States. He asked his young neighbor to be his secretary.

OREGON
COUNTRY

LOUISIANA
PURCHASE

SPANISH
POSSESSIONS

St. Louis

N

VERMONT
Part of
MA
NEW
HAMPSHIRE
MASSACHUSETTS
NEW
YORK
RHODE ISLAND
CONNECTICUT
PENNSYLVANIA
NEW JERSEY
NORTH-
WEST
TERR
DELAWARE
MARYLAND
INDIANA
TERRITORY
WEST
VIRGINIA
VIRGINIA
KENTUCKY
NORTH CAROLINA
TENNESSEE
SOUTH
CAROLINA
DISPUTED
TERRITORY
GEORGIA
MISSISSIPPI
TERRITORY
SPANISH
POSSESSIONS

**The Louisiana
Purchase**

Jefferson dreamed of a country
stretching from sea to sea. But that would
mean crossing the Louisiana Territory,
which was owned by France.

In 1803, Napoléon, ruler of France, sold
the Louisiana Territory to the United States.
Half the west now belonged to the United
States. It was time to search for a possible
water route to the Pacific Ocean, a route
known as the Northwest Passage.

A Growing Country

In 1776, patriot Thomas Jefferson wrote the Declaration of Independence. In the Declaration, the thirteen American colonies declared freedom from British rule. The colonies defeated the British in the Revolutionary War and set up their nation with its own government. The thirteen colonies became the United States of America.

Jefferson became the third president in 1801, when the United States was only twenty years old. By then the country had sixteen states: Virginia, North Carolina, South Carolina, Georgia, Tennessee, Kentucky, Pennsylvania, Maryland, Delaware, New Jersey, New York, Rhode Island, Massachusetts, Connecticut, Vermont, and New Hampshire. Jefferson hoped the United States would grow to include much more territory.

2 THE CORPS OF DISCOVERY

President Jefferson chose his secretary, Meriwether Lewis, to lead the expedition. Meriwether's experience in the army and his knowledge of the western territory would be useful. He had learned how to live in the wilderness.

The main goal was to find the Northwest Passage. Meriwether realized that one man could not lead an expedition this big. Jefferson agreed. Meriwether wrote to his old friend William Clark, inviting him along. William wrote back, "My friend, I join you with hand and heart." Meriwether and William became captains of the expedition.

Meriwether carried this watch with him during the expedition.

William Clark drew maps throughout the journey.

Meriwether got ready for the trip. He went to Pennsylvania to visit the nation's leading doctors and scientists. He learned to chart a course by the stars, to set a broken leg, and to preserve plant samples and animal skins.

He gathered supplies and picked the other men who would go with him and his friend William Clark. Jefferson named the group the Corps of Discovery.

SEARCHING FOR THE NORTHWEST PASSAGE

For over one hundred years, the Spanish, French, and British had looked for the Northwest Passage. It took ships two years to sail from North America all the way around South America to trade with China. If a river crossed the Rocky Mountains, this new route would make trade easier. But a U.S. expedition to find the passage would have been dangerous. Americans would have had to cross enemy territory. France owned the Louisiana Territory—all the land south of Canada, north of Florida, and east of the Mississippi River. The Louisiana Purchase opened the area to U.S. explorers.

In the winter of 1803, Meriwether studied Jefferson's maps of the Missouri River. The Corps would search for the beginning of this waterway. They hoped it joined the Columbia River on the other side of the Rocky Mountains.

Congress gave Meriwether $2,500 for the trip. Meriwether did not know exactly what they needed or how long they would be gone. He simply had to guess.

Merriwether bought rifles, knives, cannons, and a special airgun. He bought fishing hooks, pencils, blankets, mosquito netting, and dried soup. And he bought thirty linen shirts, six copper kettles, four tin horns, and one portable microscope.

Meriwether and William went up the Missouri River, shown here at the shore of Mandan, North Dakota.

Lewis and Clark used colored beads like these to trade with the Indians they met along their way.

For trading with Indians, he bought magnifying glasses, red silk handkerchiefs, scissors, mirrors, ribbons, beads, thimbles, and buttons.

Next Meriwether traveled to Pittsburgh to have a barge-shaped keelboat built according to his design. He also bought a black Newfoundland dog he named Seaman.

During the winter of 1803–1804, William Clark trained the men at Camp Wood, near the Missouri River. Meriwether bought more supplies in St. Louis, Missouri.

The Corps expected to be gone for about eighteen months or two years. After months and months of preparation, everyone was eager to leave. At last spring came, and it was time to begin the expedition.

Artist Thomas Mickell Burnham painted this image of Meriwether and William on their expedition.

3 UP THE MISSOURI

O n May 14, 1804, the Corps of
Discovery paddled up the Missouri
River. It was a rainy Monday afternoon, but
William Clark and his men were ready.

They picked up Meriwether Lewis in St.
Louis. Along the river, crowds cheered
when they pushed off once more. The
expedition was finally underway.

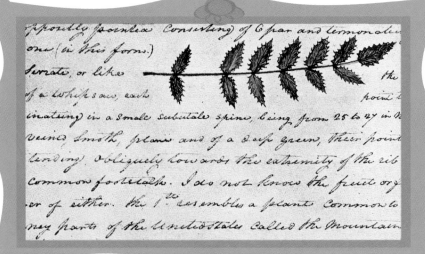

This is one of William's many sketches of plant life he saw during the expedition. He also wrote detailed notes.

Three boats carried the men, Lewis's dog, and all the supplies. Captain Lewis and Captain Clark rode in the fifty-five-foot keelboat. Others steered two dugout boats called pirogues. Besides the leaders, there were twenty-one soldiers, eleven rivermen, one interpreter, and an African American man, York, who was William's slave.

Rowing upstream was difficult. They were lucky to make fourteen miles a day. Mosquitoes bothered everyone, even Seaman. The men also got sores, snakebites, and sunstroke.

The exploration party rose at dawn every day, ate cold leftovers from the night before, packed, and "proceeded on," as Clark wrote in his journal. They did not stop for a noon meal. At the end of the day, George Drouillard, the interpreter, took some men on shore to shoot game for that night's dinner. Meriwether also walked on shore. He made careful notes about the birds, plants, animals, and even the weather.

Herds of buffalo grazed on the grasslands of the Great Plains.

In the evenings, the men relaxed around a campfire. Sometimes Pierre Cruzatte played his fiddle. The captains recorded the day's events in their journals. Then everyone fell asleep under the stars.

On July 21, the Corps reached the Platte River. They were now in the region called the Great Plains. Buffalo, elk, and antelope roamed the grassy landscape. The men called prairie dogs "barking squirrels."

Black-tailed prairie dogs make a warning call that sounds like a dog's bark.

This woodcut shows Meriwether and William meeting with the Indians at Council Bluffs.

The party stopped when they saw Oto and Missouri Indians. George Drouillard used sign language so Meriwether and the Indians could talk to each other. The captains named the site where they met the Oto and Missouri Council Bluffs.

As the journey continued, the Corps saw other tribes. The Yankton Sioux were friendly. The Teton Sioux were not.

All the Indians were curious about Meriwether's huge dog and William's slave, York. The Indians had never seen a black man before.

SEAMAN

Meriwether Lewis bought his dog, Seaman, for twenty dollars. He turned out to be well worth it. On the expedition, Seaman caught squirrels, beaver, and even an antelope. One night Seaman scared off a buffalo rushing into camp. A Shawnee Indian once offered Lewis furs for his dog, but Lewis refused. Another time, Indians tried to kidnap Seaman. The dog had a landmark named after him, Seaman Creek (now called Montana Creek).

Summer turned into fall. In late October, the expedition stopped for the winter. The men built a fort near the villages of the friendly Mandan Indians. They built eight cabins in a V-shape, surrounded by a high fence. The Mandans often visited Fort Mandan.

A French Canadian trapper named
Toussaint Charbonneau joined the Corps as
a translator. His young wife, Sacagawea,
was with him. She was a Shoshone Indian.
Sacagawea was expecting a baby.

On February 11, 1805, Sacagawea gave
birth to a boy named Jean Baptiste. William
called the baby Pompey.

The Mandan Indians lived in dome-shaped structures. The
Mandan hung utensils and weapons on beams and posts
that supported the domed roof.

When the ice on the Missouri River melted, it was time to head out again. The captains sent some soldiers and rivermen back to St. Louis in the keelboat. The Corps set off in the pirogues and six new canoes. They were entering territory where no white men had ever been before.

Besides Meriwether and William, this painting shows Sacagawea with her baby in his cradleboard and William's slave, York.

4 MEETING THE SHOSHONE

The Corps made its way to the treeless high plains. Hot winds blew sand in their faces. It was so cold at night that their moccasins froze.

At each campsite, Sacagawea set up a buffalo-hide teepee. She gathered greens and dug roots, all with her baby in a cradleboard on her back. William liked Sacagawea. She called him Red Hair.

A buffalo looks out over the Great Falls of the Missouri River, in what became the state of Montana.

The captains were surprised to discover a split in the Missouri River. Which way should they go? After exploring both forks, William and Meriwether decided on the south fork.

On June 13, the Corps reached the Great Falls the Indians at Fort Mandan had told them about. That meant William and Meriwether had made the right decision. Meriwether thought the falls were "the grandest sight I had ever beheld."

The falls were beautiful, but they were a problem. The men could not paddle over the forty-foot drop. They had to haul the boats and supplies overland.

With rough wheels attached to the canoes, the men pulled heavy loads over the rocky land. Prickly pear thorns cut their moccasins. It took a month to go around the falls. Then the expedition returned to water.

These men are portaging, or carrying, boats and supplies overland.

The Madison and Jefferson Rivers join to form the Missouri at Three Forks in Montana.

On July 27, the Corps camped at a place where the Missouri River branched into three streams. Meriwether named the place Three Forks. It was near Sacagawea's homeland.

Meriwether and a few other men found the source of the Missouri, only a small stream of water. He climbed a ridge beyond that, hoping to find the Northwest Passage. All he saw were more mountains. There was no Northwest Passage.

August 18 was Meriwether's thirty-first birthday. In his journal, he scolded himself for being "indolent," or lazy. He vowed to spend the rest of his life helping people.

The expedition needed horses to cross the Rocky Mountains. Meriwether and William counted on buying horses from the Shoshone Indians, who lived in the area.

SACAGAWEA

Sacagawea made many crucial contributions to the expedition. Once, a sudden storm knocked one of the pirogues on its side. Charbonneau got scared and let go of the rudder. Maps, notebooks, and instruments spilled into the water. Calmly, Sacagawea caught the items before they were carried downstream.

Lewis praised her quick thinking in his journal.

The Corps finally found a Shoshone camp. Sacagawea translated the talk between Meriwether and the chief. With great excitement, she suddenly realized that Chief Cameahwait was her brother! She had not seen him for many years. With Sacagawea's help, the captains traded goods for twenty-nine horses.

This painting shows Meriwether meeting the Shoshone Indians.

Fending off bears was just one of the challenges faced by Lewis and Clark on their expediton.

By then it was late August. Water froze in pans at night. The Corps needed to hurry across the mountains or risk being trapped by early snows. A Shoshone guide led the expedition over a snowy pass. The men ate the last of the salt pork and flour. There was no grass for the horses. Everyone was wet, cold, and hungry. Finally, after covering 160 miles in eleven days, they had crossed the Rockies.

OTHER MEMBERS OF THE CORPS

George Drouillard, half-Shawnee, half-French, was an expert tracker, hunter, and interpreter. He also knew Indian sign language. Pierre Cruzatte was blind in one eye. He entertained the Corps and the tribes along the way with his fiddle. Eighteen-year-old George Shannon was the youngest member. There were also two brothers in the Corps, Joseph and Reubin Field.

York, William's slave, was the only African American member of the expedition. Besides being William's companion, he helped paddle canoes, put up the teepee, and cook.

The Columbia River led the Corps to their final destination—the Pacific Ocean.

In five newly made dugout canoes, the Corps of Discovery traveled by water down the Snake River. On October 16, the party reached the Columbia River, which would lead them to the sea.

The final leg of the trip was four miles of dangerous rapids and waterfalls. The men often had to carry the supplies on land. At waterfalls, they carefully lowered the loaded canoes on elk-skin ropes.

The expedition left bare landscape behind them and entered the Pacific rain forest. Dense morning fog every day kept the men from continuing until after noon.

On November 6, 1805, after the fog had lifted, the Corps paddled west. Suddenly the men gave a glad cry. William wrote in his journal, "Ocian [ocean] in view! O! the joy."

The Columbia River Gorge is one of the many natural wonders Meriwether and William probably saw.

5 HOMEWARD BOUND

What William Clark actually saw was Gray's Bay, not the ocean. That was still twenty miles away.

But the Corps could go no farther. Wind, waves, and heavy rain drove them into a small cove for eleven days. Wet and miserable, they huddled in their rotting clothes.

The basin of the Columbia River

When the weather let up, Meriwether explored the coastline. At a place he called Cape Disappointment, he carved his initials in a tree. When William found Meriwether's initials, he carved his name and "By Land from the U. States in 1804 & 1805."

Winter was coming. It was time to think about shelter. All the members of the Corps, including Sacagawea and York, voted on where to build their fort. At this time, it was unusual for a woman or a black man to be allowed to vote. The vote showed the captains' sense of fairness.

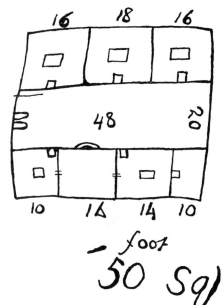

William traced this plan of Fort Clatsop on the rough elk-skin cover of his field book. The fort measured fifty feet on each side. It had three cabins along the upper wall, each with a central fireplace. Along the lower wall were four more cabins. The gates were to the left.

Fort Clatsop was finished by the end of December. After a long winter there, the Corps left Fort Clatsop on March 23, 1806. The captains knew it would take them nearly a year to get home. Would they make it with so few supplies?

Going up the Columbia River was hard. The men often towed the canoes or carried them on land. Food was scarce.

The Corps had run out of goods to trade. Instead, Meriwether and William treated sick and injured Nez Percé Indians. The other men cut brass buttons off their coats to trade for roots.

In early June, the expedition set off to cross the Rocky Mountains again. But the snow was too deep. The Corps started out again on June 25 and traveled for six days. Then the expedition split up. William took Sacagawea, Pompey, and ten men to travel down the Yellowstone River. Meriwether and his group explored the Marias River. William planned to meet Meriwether's party where the Yellowstone and Missouri Rivers joined.

When the Corps reached the Rocky Mountains, shown here, they traded their canoes to Indians for horses.

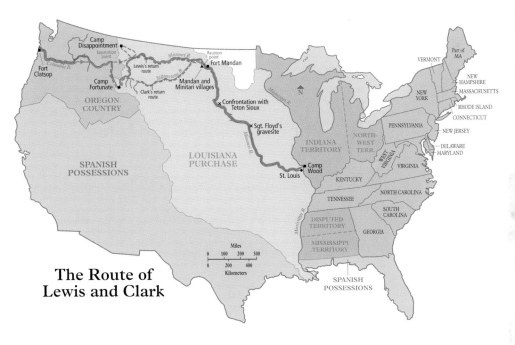

Camp
Disappointment
Separation
point
Reunion
point
Fort Mandan
Missouri R.
VERMONT
Part of
MA
Fort
Clatsop
Lewis's return
route
NEW
HAMPSHIRE
Camp
Fortunate
Clark's return
route
Mandan and
Minitari villages
NEW
YORK
MASSACHUSETTS
OREGON
COUNTRY
RHODE ISLAND
Confrontation with
Teton Sioux
CONNECTICUT
PENNSYLVANIA
NEW JERSEY
Sgt. Floyd's
gravesite
INDIANA
TERRITORY
NORTH-
WEST
TERR.
DELAWARE
MARYLAND
SPANISH
POSSESSIONS
LOUISIANA
PURCHASE
Camp
Wood
WEST
VIRGINIA
VIRGINIA
St. Louis
KENTUCKY
TENNESSEE
NORTH CAROLINA
SOUTH
CAROLINA
DISPUTED
TERRITORY
GEORGIA
Miles
0   100   200   300
MISSISSIPPI
TERRITORY
0   200   400
Kilometers
The Route of
Lewis and Clark
SPANISH
POSSESSIONS

The Route of
Lewis and Clark

William journeyed more than six
hundred miles. Meriwether rode through
the dangerous territory of the Blackfeet
Indians. Throughout the trip, Meriwether
and William named rivers, streams,
mountains, and other landmarks.

Meriwether and William met on August 12.
In dugout canoes, the Corps quickly paddled
through the Great Plains. Soon they passed
fur traders. Traders meant towns nearby.
When they saw cows grazing in fields, the
men cheered.

On September 23, 1806, the Corps of Discovery paddled into St. Louis. They had led an expedition that traveled 7,689 miles in two years, four months, and two days.

Meriwether was appointed governor of the Louisiana Territory in 1807. He was often sick and became depressed. He died of gunshot wounds on October 10, 1809. No one knows if he was murdered or if he killed himself.

William married Julia Hancock and became governor of the Missouri Territory. He was also named superintendent of Indian affairs for the U.S. government. He died on September 1, 1838.

Meriwether and William were disappointed that the Northwest Passage did not exist. But the trail they blazed became the path to the future of the United States. Through it all, Meriwether Lewis and William Clark were true friends.

TIMELINE

In the year . . .

WILLIAM CLARK WAS
BORN IN 1770.
MERIWETHER LEWIS WAS
BORN IN 1774.

1789   Clark joined the army.   `Age 19`

1794   Lewis entered the army and befriended Clark.   `Age 20`

1803   Napoléon sold the Louisiana Territory to the United States.
President Thomas Jefferson chose Lewis to lead a trip in search of the Northwest Passage.   `Age 28`
Lewis asked his old friend Clark to join him.

1804   Lewis and Clark began their expedition on May 14.   `Clark Age 34` `Lewis Age 30`
they reached the Great Plains on July 21.
they met and traded with the Oto and Missouri Indians.

1805   they first saw the Rocky Mountains on May 26.   `Clark Age 35` `Lewis Age 31`
they reached the Great Falls on June 13.
they came upon the Columbia River on October 16.
they arrived at Gray's Bay, twenty miles from the Pacific Coast, on November 6.

1806   the crew left for home on March 23.   `Clark Age 36` `Lewis Age 32`
Lewis and Clark split up on June 31.
Clark traveled the Yellowstone River.
Lewis explored the Marias River.
They met up on the Missouri, below the mouth of the Yellowstone, in August.
they paddled into St. Louis, ending the expedition, on September 23.

1807   Jefferson made Lewis governor of the Louisiana Territory.   `Age 33`
Clark was made superintendent of Indian affairs in the territory.   `Age 37`

1808	Clark married Julia Hancock.	Age 38
1809	Lewis died on October 10.	Age 35
1813	Clark was appointed governor of Missouri Territory.	Age 43
1838	Clark died on September 1.	Age 69

THE JOURNALS

William Clark kept detailed journals. This elk-skin field journal shows his careful record-keeping. This journal covers the difficult period from early September 1805 until the end of December. At that time, members of the expedition were racing against the oncoming winter. The journal contains 224 pages, nineteen maps, and some sketches. It was probably written on loose pages and bound during the winter at Fort Clatsop.

FURTHER READING

Edwards, Judith. *Lewis and Clark's Journey of Discovery.* Springfield, NJ: Enslow Publishers, Inc., 1999. The story of how Lewis and Clark overcame extraordinary obstacles to lead the expedition to the Pacific Ocean.

McGrath, Patrick. *Lewis & Clark Expedition.* Parsippany, NJ: Silver Burdett Press, 1991. A well-written account that emphasizes the success of the expedition as well as the long-term effects on Native American cultures.

Moulton, Gary. *Lewis & Clark & the Route to the Pacific.* Broomall, PA: Chelsea House, 1991. The importance of the journey is highlighted in this well-balanced history.

Sneve, Virginia Driving Hawk. *The Nez Perce.* New York: Holiday House, 1994. A beautifully illustrated book about the daily life and history of the tribe.

St. George, Judith. *Sacagawea.* New York: Putnam, 1997. The story of the expedition as seen from the eyes of the young Shoshone girl who helped guide them.

Streissguth, Tom. *Lewis and Clark: Explorers of the Northwest.* Springfield, NJ: Enslow Publishers, Inc., 1998. Traces the lives, careers, and achievements of Lewis and Clark as they explore the American Northwest territory.

WEBSITES

Lewis and Clark's Historic Trail
www.lewisclark.net
With a good selection of maps, biographies, and journal entries from the explorers, this is a great site to start the hunt for more information.

Discovering Lewis and Clark
www.lewis-clark.org
This highly interactive site brings the expedition to life with animated graphics, sound files, and a step-by-step map of the trail.

Lewis & Clark: The Journey of the Corps of Discovery
http://www.pbs.org/lewisandclark
This comprehensive site has sidenotes, documents, and images for nearly every aspect of the expedition.

SELECT BIBLIOGRAPHY

Ambrose, Stephen E. *Lewis and Clark: Voyage of Discovery.* New York: National Geographic Society, 1998.

Ambrose, Stephen E. *Undaunted Courage: Meriwether Lewis, Thomas Jefferson, and the Opening of the American West.* New York: Simon & Schuster, 1996.

Botkin, Daniel B. *Our Natural History: The Lessons of Lewis and Clark.* New York: Putnam, 1995.

DeVoto, Bernard, ed. *The Journals of Lewis and Clark.* New York: Houghton Mifflin Co., 1953.

Duncan, Dayton, and Ken Burns. *Lewis & Clark: The Journey of the Corps of Discovery.* New York: Knopf, 1997.

Gass, Patrick, and Carol Lynn MacGregor, ed. *The Journals of Patrick Gass: Member of the Lewis and Clark Expedition.* Missoula, MT: Mountain Press Publishing Co., 1997.

INDEX

Acknowledgments

For photographs and artwork: North Wind Picture Archive, front cover (both), back cover, pp. 8, 9, 20, 23, 25, 28, 29, 35, 38, 39, 45; Bryan Peterson, Legislative Media Services, p. 4; © N. Carter/North Wind Picture Archive, pp. 7, 16, 17, 21, 30; © Missouri Historical Society, p. 13; Brown Brothers, pp. 14, 26; David David Gallery, Philadelphia/SuperStock, p. 18; Superstock, pp. 22, 32, 36, 40; © Bettmann/Corbis, p. 33.
For quoted material: p. 13, Stephen E. Ambrose, *Undaunted Courage: Meriwether Lewis, Thomas Jefferson, and the Opening of the American West* (New York: Simon & Schuster, 1996); pp. 21, 22, 28, 31, 36, 42, Bernard DeVoto, ed., *The Journals of Lewis and Clark* (New York: Houghton Mifflin, 1953).